Table of contents
目錄
muk6 luk6

1. Greeting 打招呼
da2 jiu1 fu1

2. Shapes 形狀
jing4 zong6

3. Colors 顏色
ngaan4 sik1

4. Nature 大自然
daai6 ji6 yin4

5. Fruits 水果
seui2 gwo2

6. Animals 動物
dung6 mat6

7. Vegetables 蔬菜
so1 choi3

晚安！
maan5 on1

早啾！
jou2 tau2

GOOD NIGHT

Triangle
三角形
saam1 gok3 jing4

Square
正方形
zing3 fong1 jing4

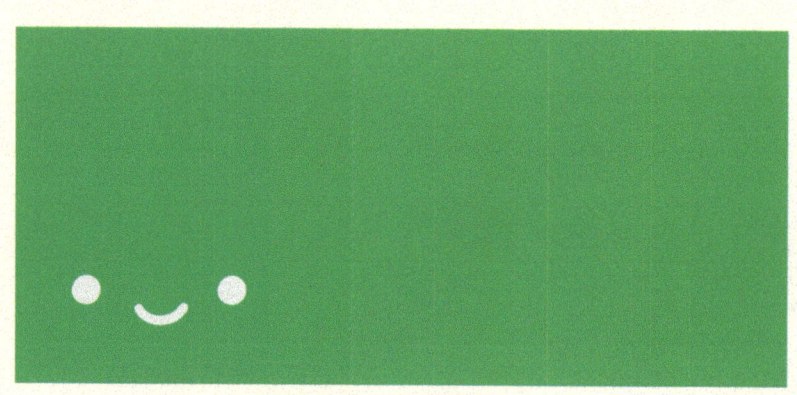

Rectangle
長方形
coeng4 fong1 jing4

Circle
圓形
jyun4 jing4

Diamond
菱形
ling4 jing4

Heart
心形
sam1 jing4

Trapezoid
梯形
tai1 jing4

Pentagon
五角形
ng5 gok3 jing4

Do you know what shape this is?
你識唔識呢個係咩形狀呀?
nei5 sik1 m4 sik1 ne1 go3 hai6 me1 jing4 zong6 aa1?

I know! This is a square.
我知啊！呢個係正方形！
ngo5 zi1 aa1！ne1 go3 hai6 zing3 fong1 jing4！

And what about this one?
咁呢個呢？
gam3 ne1 go3 ne1

I don't know, what shape is this?
我唔識呀，呢個係咩形？
ngo5 m4 sik1 aa1 ,
ne1 go3 hai6 me1 jing4 ?

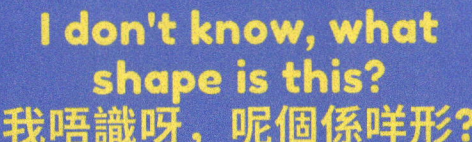

This is a triangle, it has three sides.
呢個係三角形，有三條邊。
ne1 go3 hai6 saam1 gok3 jing4 ,
jau5 saam1 tiu4 bin1

Colors
顏色
ngaan4 sik1

Purple
紫色
zi2 sik1

Brown
啡色
fe1 sik1

Grey
灰色
fui1 sik1

White
白色
baak6 sik1

Black
黑色
hak1 sik1

Gold
金色
gam1 sik1

Light Blue
淺藍色
cin2 laam4 sik1

Deep Red
深紅色
sam1 hung4 sik1

Peach Pink
桃紅色
tou4 hung4 sik1

What color do you like?
你鍾意咩顏色?
nei5 jung1 ji3 me1 ngaan4 sik1?

Sun
太陽
tai4 jyun5

Rain
雨
jyu5

Lightning
閃電
sim2 dim2

Thunder
行雷
haang4 leui4

Stars
星星
sing1 sing1

Ocean
海洋
hoi2 joeng4

Mountain
山
saan1

River
河流
ho4 lau4

Flowers
花
faa1

Tree
樹
syu6

Moon
月亮
yut6 leung6

Cloud
雲
wan4

Rainbow
彩虹
coi2 hung4

Leaf
葉
yip6

Fire
火
fo2

Night
夜晚
je6 maan5

Wind
風
fung1

Apple
蘋果
ping4 gwo2

Orange
橙
chaang2

Grape
提子
tai4 ji2

Pear
梨
lei4

Watermelon
西瓜
sai1 gwa1

Pineapple
菠蘿
bo1 lo4

Mango
芒果
mong1 gwo2

Banana
香蕉
heung1 jiu1

Blueberry
藍莓
laam4 mui2

Avocado
牛油果
ngau4 yau4 gwo2

Kiwi fruit
奇異果
kei4 yi6 gwo2

Lemon
檸檬
ning4 mung1

Peach
桃
tou4

Dragon Fruit
火龍果
fo2 lung4 gwo2

Coconut
椰子
ye4 ji2

Melon
蜜瓜
mat6 gwa1

Durian
榴槤
lau4 lin4

Grapefruit
西柚
sai1 yau2

Lime
青檸
cheng1 ning2

Strawberry
士多啤梨
si6 do1 be1 lei2

Passion fruit
熱情果
yit6 ching4 gwo2

Cherry
車厘子
che1 lei4 ji2

Fig
無花果
mou4 fa1 gwo2

Lychee
荔枝
lai6 ji1

Koala
樹熊
syu6 hung4

Fox
狐狸
wu4 lei4

Pig
豬仔
zyu1 zai2

Owl
貓頭鷹
maau1 tau4 jing1

What animal do you like?
你鍾意咩動物呀？
nei5 jung1 yi3 me1 dung6 mat6 a3?

I like dogs. They are friendly and lively.
我鍾意狗狗，佢好友善又活潑。
ngo5 jung1 yi3 gau2 gau2, keui5 hou2 yau5 sin6 yau6 wut6 put

I like cats. They are agile and well-behaved.
我鍾意貓貓，佢地好靈敏又好乖。
ngo5 jung1 yi3 maau1 maau1, keui5 dei6 hou2 ling4 man5 yau6 hou2 gwaai1

Carrot
紅蘿蔔
hung4 lo4 baat1

Cucumber
青瓜
cing1 gwaa1

Eggplant
茄子
ke4 zi2

Tomato
番茄
faan1 ke4

Broccoli
西蘭花
sai1 laan4 faa1

Onion
洋蔥
joeng4 cung1

Potato
薯仔
syu4 zai2

Green Pepper
青椒
cing1 ziu1

Lotus Root
蓮藕
lin4 ngau5

Taro
芋頭
wu6 tau4

Spinach
菠菜
bo1 coi3

Pumpkin
南瓜
naam4 gwaa1

Lettuce
生菜
sang1 coi3

Enoki Mushroom
金針菇
gam1 jam1 gu1

Green onion
蔥
chung1

Corn
粟米
suk1 mai5

Celery
西芹
sai1 kan2

Bok Choy
白菜
baak6 choi3

Mushroom
蘑菇
mo4 gu1

Garlic
蒜
syun3

Hey, what vegetables do you like?
你鍾意咩蔬菜呀?
nei5 jung1 yi3 me1 so1 choi3 aa3?

I like potatoes and broccoli. Potatoes can be made into many different dishes.
我鍾意薯仔同西蘭花，薯仔可以做成好多唔同嘅嘢。
ngo5 jung1 yi3 syu4 jai2 tung4 sai1 laan4 fa1, syu4 jai2 ho2 ji5 jou6 sing4 hou2 do1 m4 tung4 ge3 ye5

Wow, I like cucumbers and carrots. They are refreshing and nutritious.
我鍾意青瓜同紅蘿蔔，清爽又營養。
ngo5 jung1 yi3 cheng1 gwa1 tung4 hung4 lo4 baak6, ching1 song2 yau6 ying4 yeung5

Yes, vegetables are important for our health. We should eat more of them.
係呀，蔬菜對身體好重要，我哋應該食多啲。
hai2 aa3, so1 choi3 deui3 san1 tai2 hou2 jung6 yiu3, ngo5 dei6 jing1 goi1 sik6 do1 di1

www.ingramcontent.com/pod-product-compliance
Lightning Source LLC
Chambersburg PA
CBHW061122170426
43209CB00013B/1636